Still-Water Days

Still-Water Days

Poems by

Penny Harter

© 2021 Penny Harter. All rights reserved.
This material may not be reproduced in any form, published,
reprinted, recorded, performed, broadcast,
rewritten or redistributed without
the explicit permission of Penny Harter.
All such actions are strictly prohibited by law.

Cover design by Shay Culligan

ISBN: 978-1-954353-49-7

Kelsay Books
502 South 1040 East, A-119
American Fork, Utah, 84003

Acknowledgments

Poems in this collection have appeared in the following periodicals or anthologies. Most also appeared on my Facebook page and are posted in my Blog on my website pennyharterpoet.com.

Alphabet Soup: "Just Grapefruit"

Aurora & Blossoms: PoARoMo Anthology: "A Kind of Silence," "The Religion of Birds," "Whale Song"

Gatherings: "Pandemic Islands," "Pandemic Prayer"

Halfway Down the Stairs: "Topsy-Turvy"

Hedgerow Journal: "Night Coach"

Red Eft Review: "An Afternoon for Tea"

The Plague Papers: "The Marfa Lights, Marfa Texas"

Silver Birch Press: "Just Grapefruit"

Tiferet: "In Green Time"

Verse-Virtual: "Another Ordinary Day," "A Song Before Sleep," "Bittersweet," "Distant Music," "Pandemic Islands," "Pandemic Prayer," "Some Roads," "Whale Song"

Contents

Another Ordinary Day	13
Between Floors	14
Topsy-Turvy	15
Islands	16
Anything That Touches	17
All Day	19
Pandemic Prayer	20
Dandelion Puffs	21
Scoring Corona	22
In the Distance	23
The Marfa Lights, Marfa, Texas	24
Whale Song	25
Bittersweet	26
Acceptance	27
The Religion of Birds	28
Thin Places	29
The Great Blue Heron	31
Symbiosis	33
In the Shadows	34
Remembering Snow	35
Dream Flight	36
What I Learn from Birds	37
White Ibis	38
In Green Time	39
Crossing the Marsh	40
Still-Water Days	41
Some Roads	42
An Afternoon for Tea	43
Lost and Found	44
What Shall I Say?	45
The Baby Rabbit	46

Before the Naming	47
Smoke May Be Visible	48
Just Grapefruit	49
Dog Days at the Farm Stand	50
Flounder	52
Counting Game	53
Muskrat Encounter	55
Distant Music	56
Night Coach	57
Night Thoughts	58
A Song Before Sleep	59
Docking	61
Telling the Bees	62
For the New Year	63
Finding Joy in Firsts	65

Another Ordinary Day

Another ordinary day in this new pandemic world,
my only company, the television, unable to show
anything but graphs reporting rising infections,
deaths, and a government wrangling about how
to relieve a horror unthinkable before this month.

I turn it off for the night, open my bedroom window,
climb into bed and listen for the usual sound of tires
hissing on the wet road out front, but tonight I note
long pauses between cars, drift on the steady rain
into a restless sleep with dreams I can't remember.

Cardboard boxes of extra food line the edges of
the living room—a room I mostly live in these
ordinary days—and crowd my current kitchen
whose electric stove doesn't flare with the blue
gas flame that lit a former life.

Once I wrote a story called *The Family Who Lives
in the Basement.* They only came out after some
apocalypse was over, stumbling up the cellar steps,
eyes blinded by the shock of sunlight. I don't
remember what happened to them next.

I guess they adjusted, rebuilt their world best they
could, although it could not be the same as before,
no blueprints to follow, no brick and mortar waiting
in the side yard. But they went on, that I know.
Surely I would have had them go on! Surely . . .

Between Floors

In last night's dream I'm in an elevator
stuck between floors. I think I'm alone.
I don't remember the building, how long
I've been trapped, or even why I'm here.

I am getting enough oxygen through a
tubing that someone has threaded into a
corner above me, and I hear folks around
me trying to get this cage moving again.

I haven't panicked yet since I believe that
I'll be free before too long. After all, how
long can this stasis go on before I find the
right floor, see the doors safely open?

And how long before I wake up to know
that this dream is a metaphor my mind has
invented, a visual poem for how we are all
stuck in this upside-down world?

No, not upside-down—it's worse, a world
gone mad, disease and violence pushing the
brass buttons—pushing our buttons. Now
awake, I wonder whether we'll get out at all.

Yet in my dream I'm hopeful, trusting that
we won't run out of air, believing in the good
hearts of those who are working to save us,
and thankful that somehow we will survive.

Topsy-Turvy

Remember the fun of somersaults, the thrill
of rolling head-over-heels down a grassy slope?
I did it once, landing at my father's feet along
a zoo path by the caged chimps.

These days we don't roll down hills for fun,
although sometimes it feels like we're in
a zoo—or part of a visiting circus, dangling
by our knees from the trapeze bar, swinging
back and forth while the audience gasps.

The patient with lung disease is flipped
face-down to ease the pressure on the lungs,
allowing more oxygen to reach the alveoli,
the tiniest air sacs. The nurses call it proning.

As our roles in this new topsy-turvy world play
out, we know less than before which side is up,
where we are, what day it is, and even whether
we can ever find a way back.

At that long-ago zoo, my father became
a chimpanzee, grunting and gesturing at Jocko,
who answered him in kind, even flinging scat
through the bars. That's what happens when
social animals are caged. That's what they do.

Islands

We are all islands now, invisible
moats around us as we witness
the weather of our isolated lives.

It even seems there's a shift
in the light, the sky more muted
than usual, yet more blue.

Some say porpoises are frolicking
in the Venice canals, and locals
can see fish again.

This may not be true, but maybe
it is, maybe we were overdue this
reset—clearing skies over China,

most countries learning they must
help each other—though some still
refuse, hoarding their need.

Half alive, half dead, this tsunami
virus learns quickly, is speaking
to us in a new language, saying,

*time to cull the herd, to rob from
you illusion of control, and to
wake you to the energy of love.*

Anything That Touches

When one is alone and lonely, the body / gladly lingers in the wind or the rain, / or splashes into the cold river, or / pushes through the ice-crusted snow. // Anything that touches.
—Mary Oliver

One lesson in the grief support group tells us
that time, talk, tears, and touch are needed
for the healing journey.

We cry our tears, talk about our loneliness,
and share our need for loving touch as we
hug one another at the meeting's end.

Another lesson talks about how we should
seek the natural world, get out of the closed
house of our grief, tilt our faces to the sky.

Some have pets, and that helps. Some hug
pillows at night, spend hours on the phone
for the distant touch of another voice.

In childhood I discovered that when I deeply
looked at something, I was somehow touching
it—as if my eyes could tangibly feel.

Shortly after my husband died, some years
ago now, I sat on an airplane and observed
my seat mate gently stroking his wife's arm.

And I found myself folding my arms across
my lap, my left hand slowly stroking my right
forearm, unconsciously comforting myself.

In this pandemic grief-time, when so many
of us are alone in our rooms, we can go out to
touch the shining world, even in wind or rain.

Our bodies can join the family of trees, rejoice
in nearby rivers, straighten to greet the mountains,
and push through the icy crust of our isolation.

All Day

All day the silence that sounds
in these rooms lacks purpose,
flows slowly back and forth,
its tidal motion almost palpable
where dust motes float in the sun.

Those who study trees have found
that some raise and lower their
branches several times in one night,
cycling water and sugar as we do
blood and lymph, before raising
them at dawn toward the sky.

All day I have drifted through silence,
counting the hours as if they were rings
in the exposed stump of a tree brought
down by a storm to lie broken among kin,
its green leaves trembling in the wind.

Pandemic Prayer

In the one dream I remember from last night
I sit on the ground with a circle of people I know
but don't know, and feel moved to pray for two
of them, an elderly father and his grown son.

Somehow, I understand that all of us circled
around our campfire of fear need to hear good
words about these two men—that both they and
we need to remember the best of who we are.

Both prayers last long in dream-time as I
struggle to remember every good thing each
has been known for, hoping to translate years
of memories into loving words.

When I drift toward waking as the morning
sun sifts through my window blinds, I try to
retain their names—if ever I have known them—
maybe Dave and Tom? But names are gone.

Grasping the unraveling strands of my dream,
I realize I haven't known who any of us are,
and that I don't need to know. It is enough
to have prayed for them. Enough to pray.

Dandelion Puffs

The unpastured Gods have gone
—Kenneth Slessor from *Earth-Visitors*

Did the gods frequent green pastures here?
Did they press designs into our tall grasses,
taunt us with riddles hinting at their origins?

None will say they've met them face-to-face,
if faces they do have, or welcomed them to
join the daily feast at our common table.

So who created them, these visiting gods?
Who sent them to Earth, blew them out like
dandelion puffs until they landed here to

scatter fragile seed? I've not seen the dragons
they ride in on—their sudden fiery spinning in
the heavens as they come and go.

I believe that God above made these visitors—
God of all that lives on myriad unknown
planets—yet not above since there really is

no up or down, but only out from the burning
center of all birth. Someday they may return to
save us from ourselves, or perhaps to punish us

as if we were their lost children who have sadly
turned away from all we ought to love as we
spiral together through infinities of sky.

Scoring Corona

While listening to 2Cellos Play Benedictus

Long ago a friend named the cello the instrument
of compassion, its almost human voice yearning
for dialogue as it speaks to our hearts. We ache to
answer, vibrate with questions we cannot give voice.

If corona-virus could hear this cello, might it stop
ravaging us? We think it has no soul, is not a living
creature, yet it needs our cells to replicate—to make
endless armies of itself.

And if it could also hear our prayers, would it be
moved to lay down its arms, cease its assault
and leave, obedient to the plea that rises from us
in many tongues as we entreat its withdrawal?

Perhaps we need cellos in tune with this virus,
choired to penetrate corona until it resonates with
compassion, until this plague, this scourge, this
unwelcome visitor is gone.

In the Distance

In the distance someone is singing.
—Pablo Neruda; tr. W. S. Merwin

Someone is always singing, especially at
night in farmlands when the drone of the day
mutes, or in sleeping suburban neighborhoods
when a barking dog breaks the silence.

The wind plays a part, stirring summer laden
branches to whisper together, or rain to clatter
against our windows, its song a sustained chant
against drought, promising even more green.

This morning along the border of the local park,
the mallows have opened their mouths to sing
pink, fuchsia and white, their dark eyes focused
on the sun, faces nodding in the light breeze.

And someone is singing the blues from the din
of cities—distant singers unknown even to one
another. We must also heed the dissonant songs
from those sleepless neon streets.

What space separates us from someone singing?
What expanse must we traverse to find the singer
hidden among forgotten reeds, the one who dares
to try to translate the eddies of rivers between us?

How far away are those who need our love, their
distant songs wanting answer, reaching out to us
at dusk and dawn, echoing our own loneliness—
faintly calling for our antiphonal response?

The Marfa Lights, Marfa, Texas

We sit on the cold bench for hours, staring at
the darkening silhouette of the hill-line, the tower
with its flashing red warning light for planes, and
headlights snaking down the slope of the highway.

Others watchers are here—a family or two with
children and a dog, a lone hiker, all of us waiting
for the sun to set. Meanwhile, a large scorpion
appears from nowhere, a black shadow scuttling

along the seam where a low wall stands between
us and the fields that seem to go on forever. A few
children gather around it, keeping a safe distance
until they are called away.

Some say aliens are behind those flickering orbs
that fortunate folks have seen suddenly jet up
along the crest to shimmer and dance against
the night sky. People near us point to the distant

headlights casting light on the far hills, saying,
There they are! Look, right over there! They want
to believe. My eyes begin to blur from staring at
the horizon. Time to go home. No luck tonight.

We long to go beyond the world we know, want
to encounter mystery bare-handed and hope for
revelation. White light, the mystics promise
when we die. And then, what lies beyond.

Whale Song

Somewhere in an indigo ocean
a mother whale is singing love
into her newborn calf.

I swim into the video, glimpse two
ghostly figures gliding through deep
sea shadows. Her haunting cadences

wash over me, ethereal song rising
and falling in arcs that echo the flow
of slow-moving underwater waves.

I want the universe to sing like this whale.
Perhaps these creatures came here from
another galaxy, a planet made of water,

bringing with them songs of home passed
down through generations, melodies we
almost remember that call us to follow.

This ocean is twilight. The mother and
child—twin planets orbiting a single star,
and we are their moons.

Bittersweet

Every word is a container—a canoe heading
out on any waters, someone paddling it from
shore after filling it with whatever's at hand.

My canoe today is heaped with rhubarb
tempered with strawberries, like the slices
of strawberry-rhubarb pie my first husband
and I used to get for ourselves and our kids
at that little fast-food joint on Route 22—
each warm slice served in its cardboard
wedge, sweet flavor flirting with the bitter.

Break a word in half it still contains multitudes—
whoever first coupled these two words saw that
sweet must pull bitter through the rapids, help it
skirt sharp submerged rocks, never letting bitter
take the lead.

Strawberry moon tonight for those who can see
or for those who will know that it's there, even
through the storm clouds. Look for it!

Acceptance

Acceptance is a Small Quiet Room
　　　　　—Cheryl Strayed

Years ago, a wise friend asked me,
When will you learn there is no enemy?
But I was too young to understand his
question, could not begin to answer it.

Now I sit in this small room—not one
in some wooded cabin, some getaway
planted by a lake where I gently rock on
the porch and watch waterlilies open

their yellow buds under a rain-gray sky,
but here in my shelter, safe from a battle
that rages outside, listening to a hard rain
cleanse the pollen-laden air.

When will you learn there is no enemy?
I think my friend, much older than I was
then, yet younger than I am now, was
forced to find the answer when his heart

began to falter, beating ragged in his breast;
learned that we must enter the small room of
self and sit there until our spirit quiets, until
we accept what is and turn away from fear.

The Religion of Birds

> *Birds make their nests in circles, for theirs is
> the same religion as ours.*
> —Black Elk

A nest is a small circle, a sturdy room woven to
keep warm the eggs that hopefully will hatch
to birth small feathered ones with gaping beaks.

I think of the sky-blue broken pieces of a robin's
egg I picked up from the lawn some years ago,
fragments from a hatchling who had fledged.

This spring flocks of robins are everywhere,
flitting across the road, congregating on the grass
beneath the oaks, their dawn and evening songs

the lilting prayers they raise because they must.
And what of our nests, the wombs and amniotic
sacs that cradle us until we break out into air?

What songs rise within us once we've left—
songs we must give voice to even on mornings
we are tone-deaf, or evenings when we despair?

Are our beaks open, trusting nurture, seeking love?
We must look to the sky, believe in whatever spirit
animates the robins' melodies—and find our own.

Thin Places

In Celtic mythology 'thin places' exist in the universe where the visible and the invisible world come into their closest proximity, and for those that find them, they offer the clearest communication between the temporal and eternal. These thin places also include experiences people are likely to have as they encounter profound suffering, joy, and mystery.

Moments, locations, within or without the
confines of flesh and spirit, thin places call
us, whisper memories we can barely translate,
only know we need to hold them closer.

In the dark night of the bedroom, one of my
thin places wavers on the border between
sleep and waking, between dream and what
we call real—whatever real is.

Waking now and then, knowing a dream has
been seizing me, I reach for it only to feel it
drift away like smoke into a place I cannot
reenter, a portal that will only open unbidden.

Lost loved ones visit me there, pull me into
places where I feel at home although I don't
remember them. Unable to linger, I daily
seek thin places hiding in the natural world.

Time spent in communion with deer, or gazing
into a shallow roadside pond of clotted water
lilies as if it were a scrying mirror—when I enter
these still moments, a thin place embraces me.

I become deer, and even stagnant water holds
the sunning turtle who slides off the log into
the dark between yellowing lily pads that hint
at shortening daylight, cooler weather.

Along any path, thin places wait for us,
and we must seek them, must learn to slow
our pace and tame our fears until we find
ourselves between worlds, on our way home.

The Great Blue Heron

Last week, two days in a row at dusk
it was there, a motionless statue among
the many bleached stumps that jut up
from this stagnant roadside pond.

The heron's blue body stood on a ragged
root, blending in as if it were just another
dead limb in this forest of dead wood.

Some weeks earlier, I'd glimpsed a
great bird, its huge wingspan a silhouette
as it soared over the pond across the road,
one where I've seen turtles sunning on logs—
one whose waters can reflect the sky.

Then I did not know what bird it was,
almost thought I hadn't seen it at all, but
now I know it must have been this great
blue heron silently poised to spear a fish.

I stopped the car to snap a photo, hoping
to capture this holy moment out of time,
knowing that to have witnessed it once
was a gift, twice a blessing.

But this week there's no blue heron as I
daily scan the weathered stumps beneath
a gray November sky. No graceful body
teaching me to wait patiently for whatever
might surface from the dark.

It is enough to have seen it, enough to
know that for two days a great blue heron
graced this swampy pond, calling me to
pay attention, luring me out of myself.

Symbiosis

We should answer the greening oak
that calls us to sit down and lean
against its trunk, seeking wisdom.

We should witness lilacs bursting into
bloom, follow the waves of sweetness
they send out to call the bees.

Becoming oak, becoming lilac bush,
we join the greater family of those who
speak tree, those who can blossom.

In the Shadows

Despite the cooling car, today's ride is
so hot and humid that I slow down in the
shadows cast across the pebbly macadam
by tall oaks and creep along, hoping to find
again the grassy lane that runs into the woods.

Down that lane yesterday a deer stood on
spindly legs, freely nibbling fresh green shoots
along the wooded edge until she noticed that
I'd stopped to better see her. Sadly, she froze
in place to stare back, her delicate body alert.

Although I doubted the deer would reappear
today, I longed for another moment's grace that
would lead my spirit down that lane, lure me
from my time and place into deer time. And I
hoped not to frighten her.

And she was there, this time with two fawns
who seemed unafraid of my car, leaning against
her flanks. I was happy to learn that my deer
was a mother, guiding and protecting her young,
knew that was why she froze again in fear.

Remembering Snow

Waking, I open the blinds to still another
sunny summer day, yet feel oppressed by
the forecast for more heat and humidity,
a wall that will hit me if I open my door.

I remember waking to a cloud of blowing
flakes between me and the road, to snow
building beneath the empty trees whose limbs
were gathering white, to a muffling womb of
snow that sheltered where I live.

Seasons change, and despite these long hot
days of fear and hate, I am blessed to be here
at all, to have shelter, food, reasonable health,
and love of family and friends, now and in the
holdings of my heart.

Dream Flight

All those years I've dreamed of flying,
of skimming the ceiling like a human
drone, have come to this—the need to
test my wings in the morning sky.

I tell my dream-self to let me fly out my
window or pass through my bedroom walls
to coast above the nearby fields, swim in
sunlit air above a river I know is there.

I ask for a companion, not just anyone will
do, but one who flies like I can—a friend
whose spirit will soar beside me, one whom
I won't lose upon waking.

These lonely days of isolation, we crave
someone to fly with, to join us in leaving
behind locked doors that keep us from
being with those we hold dear.

It's time to flap our arms and kick our legs,
to leap from the grass, defeating gravity as
we swim our way free of it all, rise through
any clouds, and go beyond.

What I Learn from Birds

Yesterday on the road's edge
what bird lay there, body splayed
from a collision with an unexpected
obstacle? I almost stopped to confirm
that its barred feathers looked hawk.

I used to collect all manner of feathers,
lay them out on the mantel in a family
of stones and shells, and later on my
dresser at the base of the photo of my
late husband, a man who loved birds.

These days, I no longer stoop to pick up
gull, crow, blue jay, dove, or those tiny
nameless fluffs along the way. And I have
discarded many older ones—dust-gatherers
in a house already filling with dust.

Yet I still crave to feel bird-flight raise me
into the void, seek out the songs, squawks,
and cries that call me to translate—even to
chirp or whistle back as I briefly become
bird, hoping for an answer.

A simple ride with new binoculars can lift
my spirit—as a blur of white on the horizon
becomes ibis, a red flash under a black wing
shouts red-winged blackbird, and five crows
bathing in a puddle splash me with laughter.

White Ibis

White ibis, lit by summer sun, solitary bird
in the green sea of salt meadow, the stalks
of your tall red legs rise above the grasses
while the curve of your long red beak swings
back and forth, probing below the mud for tiny
crabs, fish, insects. I stop to spend time with you,
distant though you are.

Across the road, your mate shepherds three
tiny fledglings. Fiercely defending them from
a black bird that swoops down to light nearby,
she opens her wings and runs at it, scaring it off.
I remember that kind of love.

You can live sixteen years, though I suspect
you are younger than that. Yesterday my
grand-dog, a sweet golden retriever, died
of cancer. He made it to ten and one-half,
then let go. That may be why I stopped today
to be with you, white ibis, your shining white
grace against the blue sky comforting me.

There is grace all around us, even in the face
of loss, of fear, of memories that flow like the
brackish streams rippling through this marsh.

Grace all around us even in sorrow, which
today I give to this wind that just now arrives
with its cleansing salt spray from the bay—
a blessing for us both, white ibis, and beyond.

In Green Time

Each day green riots more and more
along the roadsides, threatening to
overwhelm my view into the woods
with tangles of shrub oak, laurel, and
burgeoning blueberry bushes.

Further on, the green wall of reeds has
grown so tall I can't see through them to
the endless stretch of grass that used to
host white ibis, or the horizon of bay
water glinting blue in the summer sun.

Closer to home, this afternoon's mallow
blossoms along the edge of the park have
already begun to fold inward, drooping
from heat or drought. They close at night
yet daily open pastel faces to the dawn.

A few days ago on my daughter's birthday
I dared to enter her house, pandemic mask
in place, sat at table in front of a bouquet
of roses from her husband, their red ruffles
shouting beauty in the midst of isolation.

These long hot days, even as daylight has
already begun to shorten toward autumnal
dark and chill, this part of the planet doesn't
care, is too busy making everything green
while it can. And we must do the same.

Crossing the Marsh

ripples cross
the surface of the pond—
taking me with them

a strange seabird
turns its head to stare
back at me—
waves slap against
the old pilings

marsh-flies
speckle the closed
car window—
how many days now
behind glass

again today
flocking crows blacken
that house roof—
summer rental still
unoccupied

night by night
strange dreams surface—
I wake craving change

sudden downpour—
rain so dense I stop the car
just to be in it

*having no destination
I am never lost—*
of course, and yet . . .

Still-Water Days

I row out on still waters to gather clouds,
net them in my old fishing seine and stow
them in my trusty canoe for when I might
need them on a day too bright to see.

I gather clouds from blue waters, fill the
chambers of my heart with gentle murmurs,
find comfort in their slow shape-shifting
that mirrors my own, these still-water days.

Some Roads

Some roads go nowhere—or seem to go on forever
their brown dirt and gravel spinning up under my
wheels, green-head flies battering my windows.

Some roads seem to go nowhere. *Be here now,*
swampy tangles remind me. Look at the wild black
berries not yet ripe, vines entwining dense shrubs.

I have chanced on this road today, seeking escape
from the nowhere I've been in, from tangled days
that never seem to ripen.

Be here now, though the light is waning and
the road I have taken stretches out ahead of me,
perspective narrowing to a distant dark point.

This is the road I'm on now—my random impulse
luring me deeper into the illusion of no escape—into
this fairytale woods that would swallow me whole.

Every so often another dirt road intersects, beckoning
me to turn off and try it, hoping it might lead me out,
not strand me among the pinewoods ghosts.

At last I see a highway ahead, a paved promise of
release after all—yet coupled with relief, I feel
a strange reluctance to let go of being lost.

An Afternoon for Tea

This is an afternoon for tea—
rich red Strawberry Hibiscus
deepening in a brown ceramic cup.

I delight in dunking my teabag
up and down, lowering my face
into the rising steam's sweet scent.

On today's escape from shelter I ride
through a graveyard, some stones so
old their dates are half-eroded.

A light rain begins to fall, darkening
the pebbled road, nurturing the newly
springing grass between the plots.

Years ago at my mother's memorial
gathering, my toddler granddaughter
perched on someone's marker, singing.

I hadn't thought of that for years, but
some roads take us back, even when
they wind through greening trees.

Home again, an afternoon for tea, hands
clasped around the cup's kind warmth—
blessed comfort sheltered from the rain.

Lost and Found

If you get lost on winding country roads,
driving between miles of wild blueberries,
of laurel on the verge of spilling its shining
groves of pink and white beneath the neon
green of just born leaves, you may be startled
by a dark animal ahead, a turkey vulture wise

enough to strut into the roadside undergrowth
as your car creeps near, then return to its purpose
after you pass—a flattened snake gray on the
pavement, the river of its body open and drying
in the sun, its spirit having shed its wounded
scales and slithered free.

And now a deer is crossing in the distance,
just beside an oak trunk on the left that the sun
has painted with a brilliant slash. You slow
down to peer into the dappled woods, but see
no deer—though it may still be there hidden
among dense thickets.

You think this is the middle of nowhere, feel
lost in the meanders your spirit has led you on,
yet found in the sudden revelations of these
seldom observed lives beyond your own.

What Shall I Say?

What shall I say to the two tiny fawns
grazing on soft grass along the roadside
until startled by my slowing car?

How can I follow them as they dart away
into a dense green cathedral? Although
they are old enough to be out here alone,

their mother is probably nearby, hidden
among thickets. Reading *Bambi's Mother*
as a child, I cried, learning early the sudden

pain of virtual grief, though not yet the anguish
of real loss. If I could follow these fawns, I'd
tell them they are blessed to have been born,

blessed to be bound by a protected woods
bordering a seldom-traveled road, blessed
to join the family of deer.

Yesterday, some among the five distant deer
I saw together in a deer heaven—that endless
grassy lane bordered by another protected woods

out of some long ago fairytale—knew when I had
stopped to view them, lifted their heads to stare
back at me until, sensing no danger, they resumed

peaceful grazing. Would we could be like those
deer—face what might harm us, then find within
ourselves a grassy lane where we can safely graze.

The Baby Rabbit

Today as I'm walking in from the parking
lot to my front door, a baby rabbit jumps
out of the grass as if to cross the sidewalk
before me, then pauses on the edge and
stays there for a while, not freezing in
place as an older rabbit might do, just
gazing my way as I slowly inch nearer.

So tiny, just the size to fit my palm, it
calls my hand to hold it, my fingers to
stroke its soft gray fur, raise it to my cheek.
When I get too close, it wakes from its
seeming dream to quickly hop across and
disappear into the density of a hedge-like
bush encroaching on the path.

What is it about the young of any species
that catches at our hearts? Perhaps it is the
promise of possibility—memories of the
children we once were, or of babies cradled
in our arms—of those halcyon days before
we grew to understand what seasons are,
and what they might yet be.

Before the Naming

Yesterday I met some unknown flowers blooming
along the foundation of the neighboring condo—
the former home of an old woman who died some
years ago. I'd never noticed them before, though I've
lived here a decade, never witnessed their blossoms.

Like an aging nature spirit, a woodland wise-woman,
my neighbor tended her garden as if each species were
her child. She even rescued the tiny, failing rosebush
given to me when my husband died, found for it the
fertile, sunny corner where it thrived.

She planted her flowers, and they endure though she
is gone into a wicker casket strewn with roses, given
a green burial bordering the woods. Yesterday, I could
not name those pink and white pitchers, but today
I find them in a photograph, name them calla lilies.

Before the naming, seeing. Before the seeing, pausing
long enough to be there, to slowly approach whatever
is calling you into its family, and then to listen for what
it has to tell you—perhaps a name it has given itself,
or the name it has chosen for you.

Smoke May Be Visible

The blinking neon sign along the highway
that warns *Smoke May be Visible* seems
alien, a sign left over from some previous
universe of frequent pollution.

Yet this afternoon, car windows closed,
soon I encounter it—an acrid haze which
finds its way through the cracks to sting
my eyes, irritate my throat.

Despite the smoke, it has been a gorgeous
drive, chill gusts of wind whipping the treetops,
puffy white clouds scudding in a sky so blue
I'd almost forgotten it could clear this way.

Sometimes, driving through a well-known area,
I shift my perception of the usual to view the
landscape scrolling by as if it were a place I've
never been, where every tree shines newborn.

This lockdown time, we should safely venture
out to practice *seeing,* escape the confines of
the familiar, and rinse our vision with gratitude
as we witness the unfolding of each day.

Just Grapefruit

Carefully, I place half a grapefruit
into the small white bowl that fits
it perfectly, use the brown-handled
serrated knife to cut around the rim,
separate the sections.

The first bite is neither sweet nor bitter,
but I drag a drop or two of honey around
the top, love how it glazes each pink piece,
then seeps between dividing membranes.

Pale seeds pop up from their snug burial
in the center hole, and when I'm finished,
I squeeze sticky juice from the spent rind
and drink it down.

Each grapefruit is an offering, its bright
flesh startling my fasting tongue. When
bitterness spills from the morning news,
I temper it with grapefruit, savor hidden
gifts as I slice it open, free each glistening
segment, and enter honeyed grapefruit time.

Dog Days at the Farm Stand

Dog Days: the sultry part of the summer, supposed to occur during the period that Sirius, the Dog Star, rises at the same time as the sun, the hottest time of the year in ancient Greece, a time that could bring fever or disaster. A period marked by lethargy, inactivity, or indolence.

As I pull in, I notice in the car next to
mine a barking white poodle, and I worry
about him in the heat, then note the dog's
owners have left the car's air-conditioning
on while they harvest the many bins.

This farmer grows it all on his own fields
which stretch out behind this elongated shed—
acres of corn, tomatoes, green beans, cabbage,
cucumbers, basil, peppers, and more—his
tables overflowing with succulent summer.

And at the end of the wooden stands, bakery
shelves behind glass display muffin-tops,
fresh blueberry pies, turnovers. I succumb to
a cranberry-orange muffin-top, plan to eat it
in the car before I even get home.

It's a surreal scene, rows of masked people
wandering up and down the aisles, served
by masked teenagers toting up the costs
with a pencil on a little pad. No high-tech
here except for the charge-card skimmer.

Suddenly it's August, and we have plunged
into the dog-days—not named as I thought for
the days overheated dogs lie around panting on
lawns or driveways, but rooted in the ancient
Greek beliefs about Sirius rising in the heavens.

Fever, disaster, lethargy, inactivity, or indolence—
yes, all of these are with us this pandemic summer,
yet home now, I unload my fresh corn, green beans,
Jersey tomatoes, and cucumbers, and rejoice as I
shuck my two young ears of sweet white corn!

Flounder

What is flounder watching for with its two
eyes as it lies on the seabed? Food? Predators?
What are we watching for as we flounder
week after week, some of us trapped under
fear or hopelessness? Sometimes I've leaned
into grief, been flattened by depression.

Today I almost wish I were a flounder, safe
in the sea unless eaten or caught. I'd drift to
the rhythm of predictable tides, possibly not
knowing that I am fish, not knowing I am
finite, mortal. Last night I ate my filet coated
with flavored flour, crunchy breadcrumbs.

Savoring its fresh-caught taste, I found myself
a child again at the long table in our family
beach cottage, my father heaping platters with
fresh fish and corn, coleslaw, Jersey tomatoes,
and cornbread. We ate to the sough of the surf
and the night sea breeze salting the air.

Tonight I will repeat that meal. The leftover
flounder is warming in the oven, the corn
reheating in a big pot. When we feel ourselves
floundering, perhaps we can find comfort in
remembering good times, knowing we ride
these waves together, regardless of the tide.

Counting Game

On the way to summer vacations, after my father
had loaded the car up, my sister and I climbed into
the back seat of our old Buick wagon and began the
trip to Barnegat Light on Long Beach Island, NJ.

To make the time pass, we played the animal
counting game, she staring out her window and I
out mine: so many points per horse or cow, flock
of sheep or chickens—even dogs or cats.

These days when my daily drive out of isolation
feels much the same, no *Are we there yet?*
drags my minutes, but I need a purpose as I go,
need to witness other lives beyond my own.

Yesterday's tally included eight horses, a field of
sheep—too many to accurately count—and one
chipmunk scurrying across the road. I looked for
the usual deer, but it was too hot for them.

When a child, I used to pretend I could talk with
any animal, and they would answer. Those days I
believed in magic, often fell asleep dreaming of a
tree-trunk doorway into an undiscovered country.

I imagined touching the hidden pattern only I could
find in the rough bark of an old oak, and when its
door opened, I'd step over the sill into a radiant
fairyland where kindly magic folk greeted me.

As I scan for deer on my frequent rides down roads that run between patches of dense woods, I'm still playing the counting game—and I want to believe my oak is really out there, waiting to welcome us all.

Muskrat Encounter

On yesterday's ride when I stopped by a small, historic country church, a scared muskrat waddling on the driveway suddenly scrambled into a hole in the stone foundation.

childhood memories
of houses that were mine—
ghosts in the windows

Wild muskrats usually live no more than about three years. The swampy woods and river around that church make it prime muskrat territory.

My father's uncles down in the Carolina swamps wore coonskin caps. I knew those caps were from raccoons they killed themselves, skinned, ate, and wore. How sanitized my life is, especially now when picking up boxed, canned, or shrink-wrapped food in a market parking lot.

skin-a-rabbit
my mother said when she
pulled off my tee-shirt

With pandemic time at hand, I have now met muskrat, not as delicate and alluring a species as the deer I've loved seeing, yet here among us, sharing territory with our species.

returned long ago
that vintage fur coat found
in a thrift store

Distant Music

Childhood is the kingdom where nobody dies.
  —Edna St. Vincent Millay

Traveling on the wind distant music chiming
from the coming ice-cream truck brings me
good humor—almond-crunch-vanilla popsicle
laughter dripping down my chin those long
gone summer evenings.

I sit on our old stone steps, eagerly waiting
for the magic man to stop in front, open the
small square door, let out a puff of frozen
smoking air, and plunge his hand in to pull
out any favorites we children clamor for.

Who are the others waiting with me in that
kingdom lost to decades now, shadowy figures
leaping on the edge of dusk? *Childhood is the
kingdom where nobody dies*? For some that may
be true, but sometimes they do die, you know—

pets, parents, grandparents, even classmates
here one day, gone the next. Yet in the endless
summers of that kingdom, ice-cream always
comes to us on time, promising a treat we can
savor before dark—before it can melt away.

Night Coach

getting my father
off the train from New York—
great clouds of steam

childhood memory
of a trip I never made—
or did I?

dining car—
the charm of white linen
and silver utensils

at each crossroad
bells and whistles—
strangers wave

night coach—
my reflected face a ghost
in the window

cross-country train—
no way to lie down
on economy seats

waking at night
to a faraway whistle—
I ride the dark

Night Thoughts

All the soarings of my mind begin in my blood.
                              —Rainer Maria Rilke

Toward dawn last night, my left ear on the
pillow caught the slow beating of my heart,
a calm, persistent whooshing in my skull.

I shifted my position to lessen it a bit but
still that steady rhythm kept me awake, tuned
to the organ that began its work long months

before my birth. Night thoughts, some call
these visitations that find us in the dark—
memories stored in the heart's brain cells,

each cell holding its own. I should listen
unafraid to this companion who keeps me
living while it can. Whether curled around

another whom I love, or pulling close
the covers for their warmth, I honor the
bloodlines that have brought me here,

this faithful heart that lets me fall asleep
again, wake again, stretch to greet the
morning, breathe deeply, and rise.

A Song Before Sleep

I would like to sing someone to sleep
—Ranier Maria Rilke, *To Say Before Sleep*

I think it will be a song without words,
or perhaps a song in a language I invent,
a gently babbling stream.

If I can open the mouth of my heart, my
hope chest of memory, perhaps a chant
I learned by heart and sang at evensong
in some lost monastic life will find voice
and rise to comfort both myself and you.

I may merely hum, voice vibrating deep
in my chest as I follow the thread of a
familiar melody I can't quite recall—
maybe the one I hummed years ago to
my infant grandson while holding a
nebulizer over his nose and mouth and
rocking us both until he hummed back.

If my song does find words, may they
be words that cradle you as you drift
through the twilight door that swings
between day and dark; may they be balm
to your spirit, soothing you as if you were
a child again, your head on my shoulder.

And may your breathing time to mine as you
find the deep room of sleep and stay there
although the wind moans in the eaves, blowing
night rain against your windows.

And even when thunder knocks hard at your dreams, know that it, too, is simply raising its own wordless song.

Docking

This morning two astronauts docked
with the space station. Far above Earth's
blessings, freed from our current crises,
they are safely sheltered.

Down here, we are adrift, can't seem to find
the way to our dock just yet.

Remember that poster on the classroom wall—
the one with the arrow pointing to a small blue
dot, its adjacent text stating, *You are Here?*

Remember the immeasurable distance surrounding
that lonely planet? We need to discover how to
dock, need to see that poster again, remind ourselves
that *We are Here. We are Here. We are all Here.*

Telling the Bees

In rural Britain, the bees were to be told of deaths and all important family matters, including births, marriages, and long absences due to journeys. If the bees were not told, all sorts of calamities might happen. Bees were also known as the link between our world and the spirit world, so telling them might carry messages to the dead.

Recently a truck carrying hives crashed,
spilling broken hive boxes and bees across
the highway. Beekeepers from all around
rushed to salvage and relocate survivors.

What shall we now be telling the bees
as they retreat to their hives for the winter,
begin to form a ball and vibrate their wings
to keep the whole community warm?

We can tell them of those we've lost to
the virus that caused us to crash, tell of
how we are faring in our broken hives
without the usual company of family

and friends—of how some of us will have
to keep ourselves warm in the coming cold.
We can ask them who will salvage us,
rehouse us in the months ahead?

Yet we must also remember to tell them
of the good things—births, marriages, even
the random small moments of celebration
that can still illuminate our dark times.

For the New Year

On this first day of the new year, may all
the birds I remember coming to the two
feeders we hung from the branches of the
Russian Olive near that long ago window

gather again here under this dawning sky
to enjoy suet, sunflower seeds, and millet.
I can't recall the name of the store where we
got the bags of birdseed, but I do recall the

pleasure you took in filling the feeders,
defeating the wily squirrels, and our rare
glimpse of a red fox running alongside the
tracks behind the house as we watched the

constant fluttering of sparrows and finches.
And then came the flickers, those gorgeous
visitors who suddenly blessed our yard with
their red caps and brilliant speckled plumage.

On this first day of the new year, I'm feeding
too, pecking at seeds of the past, discarding
hulls that fell to lie on the snow or in the winter
pale grass, my time caught in bird-time as I

celebrate both what was and what is, winging
forward through those years to this life now,
the one where a flock of cardinals darts across
the road to light on the barren limbs of a family

of scrub oak—small scarlet harbingers whose
wings raise the dead brown leaves still clinging
to their cold branches into the dawning light
of this new year, ringing in hope.

Finding Joy in Firsts

First time in a restaurant in a year,
I celebrate their *Special:* corned beef,
cabbage, potatoes, chunky carrots, and
grainy spicy mustard in its tiny cup.

And I'd almost forgotten the moist
delight of fresh cheese-bread. Other
diners sit at distanced tables, masks off
as they savor their mutual meals.

First time in a thrift shop in a year,
I quickly remember its layout—where
to find long-sleeved shirts, jeans, and
the best aisles for random wandering.

First time in more than a year to visit
the ocean, but yesterday I find it again,
its wide blue horizon opening my heart
as I breathe in salty winds.

It's been a year since the clutch of
small daffodils poked out from behind
the base of the drainpipe, and here
they are again, squashed but whole,

kind of like we are now, emerging
from the dark ground of a pandemic
year, looking for signs of spring like
my late husband sought bluebirds.

And after too many silent weeks, this
poem's blooming, too, born from the
gift of vaccination, yesterday's cloudless
blue, and a robin's morning song.

About the Author

Penny Harter lives in Mays Landing, NJ. Her poems have been published widely in journals and anthologies, and her literary autobiography appears as an extended essay in *Contemporary Authors Autobiography Series, Volume 28* (1998) as well as in *Contemporary Authors, Volume 172* (1999). A poem of hers was featured in *American Life in Poetry*, and journals such as *Persimmon Tree, Rattle, Tattoo Highway, Tiferet,* and *Windhover* have published her work.

Recent poems appear in the anthologies *Poetry of Presence, The Book of Donuts, Healing the Divide,* and *How to Love the World: Poems of Gratitude and Hope.* Her essays and poems also appear in the writing guides *Wingbeats: Exercises & Practice in Poetry, The Crafty Poet: A Portable Workshop, The Crafty Poet II,* and *The Practice of Poetry* (Terrapin Books).

Her most recent books include *A Prayer the Body Makes, The Resonance Around Us, One Bowl, Recycling Starlight,* and *The Night Marsh.* With her late husband William J. Higginson, she co-authored *The Haiku Handbook* (25th Anniversary Edition, 2010).

Harter was a featured reader at the 2010 Geraldine R. Dodge Poetry Festival and has won three poetry fellowships from the New Jersey State Council on the Arts, awards from the Geraldine R. Dodge Foundation, the Mary Carolyn Davies Award from the Poetry Society of America, the first William O. Douglas Nature Writing Award for her work in *American Nature Writing*, 2002, and two residencies from Virginia Center for the Creative Arts.

www.ingramcontent.com/pod-product-compliance
Lightning Source LLC
Chambersburg PA
CBHW021026090426
42738CB00007B/916